Diabetes

30-Day Keto Diet Recipes & Meal Plans

Sarah Underwood

The material on this book is for informational purposes only. As each individual situation is unique, you should use proper discretion, in consultation with a health care practitioner, before undertaking the protocols, diet, exercises, techniques, training methods, or otherwise described herein. The author and publisher expressly disclaim responsibility for any adverse effects that may result from the use or application of the information contained herein.

Disclaimer

The author does not guarantee that any information, products or recommendations will provide you with the same benefits that she has achieved. This book is sold with the understanding that the author and publisher of this book are not engaged in any legal, medical or professional advice. If legal or medical expertise is required, the services of a competent professional should be sought. Neither the author nor the publisher is a medical practitioner. The author and publisher shall have neither liability nor responsibility to any person, company or entity with respect to any loss or damage caused directly or indirectly by the concepts, ideas and information presented in this book.

Sarah Underwood (March,2017).
30-Day Keto Diet Recipes & Meal Plans

Table of Contents

30-Day Ketogenic Meal Plan For Diabetes

What is a ketogenic diet?

A ketogenic diet is a way of eating that is very low in carbohydrates. Reducing carbs changes the body's metabolism and is perfect for easy weight loss. The metabolic process burns fat when it doesn't have enough carbohydrates. There are, however, many more important benefits.

The ketogenic diet limits the amounts of grains, starches and sugars that are consumed and fuels your body with fat. This reduced insulin levels and lets fat burn much more efficiently. In a 2003 study, participants using a ketogenic diet lost more than twice the weight than participants that restricted calories. One of the reasons for this rapid weight loss is that the ketogenic diet replicates the state of fasting. A fasting person burns fat, and the ketogenic diet derives its energy primarily from burned fat. The typical ketogenic diet gets 70 percent of calories from fat, 20 percent of calories from protein, and 5 percent of calories from carbohydrates.

What are the benefits of going on a Ketogenic Diet?

The concept of a low-carb and high fat diet has been studied since the 1980s and has been shown to be tasty and very effective in the treatment of a number of diseases.

1. In over 20 studies, low-carb diets resulted in greater weight loss and improvements of cholesterol levels.

2. A major problem with most diets is hunger. People are simply miserable and hungry much of the time. That's why so many diets fail. A low-carb diet, however, is naturally filling and naturally reduces the appetite. When people eat less carbohydrates and more fats and protein, they actually eat fewer calories without counting them. Weight loss happens without effort. Eating low-carb should become a lifestyle instead of a diet.

3. Stomach weight can be a problem even for otherwise slender people. The stomach is where fat is kept and stored. A low-carb diet can proportionately reduce fat in the abdomen. This can lead to a reduction of type 2 diabetes and the risk of heart problems.

4. Doctors keep wanting to check their patients' triglycerides, and lots of people don't even know what those triglycerides are. Basically, they are fat groups, and too many of them can raise the chances of stroke. What elevates the triglyceride levels are carbohydrates. By reducing carbohydrates, people tend to lower the amount of triglyceride in the blood.

5. Carbohydrates break down to simple sugars inside our body and raise our level of blood sugar. When this happens, it can result in type 2 diabetes.

6. A low-carb diet can lower blood pressure. High blood pressure is the starting point of many diseases, such

as stroke, heart disease, kidney problems, and others. By lowering carb intake, the risk of these diseases is considerably lowered.

7. John Hopkins University has been doing extensive research on the effects of a ketogenic diet on seizures. It's been shown that among children, a ketogenic diet resulted in 50 percent less seizures, and more than 15 percent of the patients ended up with no seizures. Studies are now being conducted on the effects of a ketogenic lifestyle on Parkinson and Alzheimer's patients.

I know how challenging it may be for someone to plan healthy meals especially for someone with diabetes. This is the reason I've written this book to help eliminate the frustration and boredom that may come with someone new to ketogenic diet. Please keep in mind that ketogenic diets may not work for everyone with type 2 diabetes as every person's body is different and your blood glucose level may respond differently to ketogenic diet.

It is extremely to continue to monitor your blood sugar levels throughout the day while on ketogenic diet to make sure they are within target range. You should always consult with your physician prior to starting any new diets.

Day 1

(Daily: 1600 calories, 136g fat, 12g carbs, 85g protein)

Breakfast:

Bacon and Spinach Frittata

2 servings

Ingredients

- 4 slices bacon
- 1 package chopped and drained frozen spinach
- ½ cup feta cheese
- 10 eggs
- ½ cup heavy cream
- ½ cup whole milk
- Salt and pepper to taste
- Dash of nutmeg

Directions:

1. Fry the bacon in a skillet and drain the fat.
2. Crumble the bacon into pieces and place in a bowl. Add the feta cheese and mix.
3. Transfer the mixture to a greased baking dish.
4. Combine the remaining ingredients until they are well blended.
5. Pour the egg mix over the bacon.
6. Bake for 45-50 minutes at 375 degrees.

Note: Make enough bacon for lunch

Lunch

Egg Salad

Ingredients

- 5 large eggs
- 3 tablespoons mayonnaise
- 1 teaspoon lemon juice
- 1 teaspoon mustard
- Salt and pepper to taste

Directions:

1. Fill a pan with water and add the eggs.
2. Let the eggs cook for 10 minutes.
3. Allow the eggs to cool before peeling.
4. Chop the eggs (by hand or a food processor).
5. Stir in the remaining ingredients. Add the bacon if you made enough for breakfast.
6. Serve on a plate of lettuce.

Dinner

Cauliflower Gratin

Ingredients:

- 4 cups uncooked cauliflower florets
- 3 tablespoons butter
- ¼ cup half & half or heavy cream
- 5 pepper jack cheese slices

- Salt and pepper to taste

Directions:

1. Cook the cauliflower in a pan until done.
2. Drain the water from the paper and add the butter, half & half, salt and pepper.
3. Stir and cook on low for 5 minutes.
4. Place the cauliflower in a baking dish and top with the heavy cream and cheese slices.
5. Bake at 350 degrees for 10 minutes or until cheese has melted.

Day 2

(Daily: 1330 calories, 108g fat, 9g carbs, 75g protein)

Breakfast

Spinach Omelet

Ingredients:

- 2 large eggs
- 2 tablespoons milk
- ½ cup diced tomato
- 1 cup drained and shredded frozen spinach
- 2 tablespoons diced onions
- 2 tablespoons butter

Directions:

1. Melt the butter in a skillet.
2. Combine the eggs and the milk with a whisk.
3. On low heat, cook the eggs until almost firm
4. Add the tomatoes, spinach and onions.
5. Fold one half of the omelet over the other.
6. Serve with berries and a banana.

Lunch

Cobb Salad

1 serving

Ingredients for Dressing

- ½ tablespoons of olive oil
- ½ tablespoon apple cider vinegar
- 1 teaspoon of Dijon mustard
- ¼ teaspoon minced garlic
- Salt and pepper to taste

Ingredients for Cobb Salad:

- ½ cup of sliced ham
- ¼ cup diced tomatoes
- 2 tablespoons blue cheese
- 1 sliced hard-boiled egg
- 2 cups chopped romaine lettuce
- 4 avocado dices
- 2 bacon slices

Directions:

1. Place the lettuce on a plate.
2. Add the egg slices, blue cheese, cubed ham, bacon and avocado slices in neat rows.
3. Whisk together the dressing ingredients and drizzle over salad.

Dinner

Chicken in Creamy Sauce

4 servings

Ingredients:

- 1 lb. chicken thighs (please don't use breast meat)
- 2 tablespoon olive oil
- 1 cup chicken broth
- 1 cup heavy cream
- 1 teaspoon oregano
- 2 cups kale (you can use spinach)
- 2 tablespoon butter
- 3 tablespoons almond flour
- Salt and pepper to taste

Directions:

1. On medium heat, add the oil to a skillet.
2. Salt and pepper the chicken thighs and brown them in the skillet.
3. Cook the thighs until they are done.
4. While the chicken is cooking, heat the butter in another pan. When the butter is hot, stir in the flour. Keep stirring to create a paste (roux).
5. Slowly add the cream and keep stirring until the cream reaches the boiling point.
6. Add the broth and the oregano and lower the heat
7. Cook for 5 minutes.
8. Transfer the chicken thighs to a platter. Pour the sauce into the empty skillet and deglaze.
9. Add the kale and combine with the sauce.
10. Spoon the kale and sauce over the chicken.

Day 3

(Daily: 1288 calories, 78g fat, 5.9g carbs, 76.6g protein)

Breakfast

Bacon and Eggs:

For perfectly fluffy eggs, use a spatula to keep them moving and stirred.

Ingredients:

- 3 large eggs
- 2 slices bacon
- 1 tablespoon milk or cream
- Salt and pepper to taste
- 1 tablespoon butter

Directions:

1. In a skillet, fry 2 slices of bacon.
2. Whisk the eggs and milk together in a bowl.
3. In a second skillet, melt the butter.
4. Keep the heat low and pour in the eggs.
5. Use a spatula to keep shifting the eggs to the middle.
6. Cook for about 3 minutes. Add the salt and pepper.

Lunch

Steak Salad

Ingredients:

- ½ lb. steak
- 2 cups spinach
- 8 halved cherry tomatoes
- ½ cup sliced and seeded bell pepper
- 3 thinly sliced radishes
- 1 tablespoon olive oil
- 1 tablespoon juice of a fresh lemon juice
- Salt and pepper to taste
- ¼ cup soy sauce
- Extra olive oil for cooking

Directions:

1. Place the steak and soy sauce in a bowl or ziplock bag and refrigerate for at least 2 hours.
2. Combine the spinach, bell peppers, radishes and tomatoes in a large bowl.
3. Drizzle with the lemon juice and olive oil and toss. Season with the salt and pepper.
4. Transfer the salad unto 2 plates in equal amounts.
5. Toss the marinade.
6. Heat the olive oil in a skillet and prepare the steak to preferred doneness.
7. Slice the steak and top each salad plate with the slices.

Dinner

Seared Cod

4 servings

Ingredients:

- 4 cod filets
- 4 tablespoons butter (or you can use ghee)
- 5 minced garlic cloves
- A dash of salt

Directions:

1. Melt the butter in a skillet.
2. Sauté the garlic for 5 minutes.
3. Transfer the filets to the skillet and add the salt.
4. The fish will turn white as it cooks. Turn the cod over when the filets are halfway done, about 5 minutes.
5. Continue cooking until the filets are solid white and flaky.
6. Transfer the cod to a platter and drizzle with the butter and garlic from the skillet.
7. Serve with sliced tomatoes drizzled with a teaspoon of olive oil and a dash of salt.

Day 4

(Daily: 1522 calories, 112g fat, 15.5g net carbs, 83g protein)

Breakfast

Cream Cheese Pancakes

1 serving

Ingredients:

- 2 oz. cream cheese
- 2 large eggs
- 1 teaspoon honey
- ½ teaspoon cinnamon
- 2 tablespoons of butter

Directions:

1. Combine all of the ingredients except the butter, either with a whisk or in a blender. The batter should be nice and smooth.
2. Melt the butter in a skillet.
3. Pour 2 tablespoons of batter into the skillet and cook the pancake until golden brown, about 2 minutes.
4. Turn the pancake and cook for another minute.
5. Repeat this with the remaining batter.
6. Top the pancakes with syrup and seasonal berries.
7. Serve with 2 slices of prepared bacon

Lunch

Cauliflower Salad and Meatballs

Ingredients for Cauliflower Salad

- 2 cups uncooked cauliflower florets
- ½ cup chopped red cabbage
- ¾ cup chopped artichoke hearts (packed in water, not oil)
- ⅓ cup grated parmesan cheese
- ⅓ cup chopped basil
- 2 tablespoons chopped sundried tomatoes
- 2 tablespoons chopped black olives, preferable Kalamata
- 1 minced garlic clove
- 2 tablespoons balsamic vinegar
- 3 tablespoons good quality olive oil
- Salt and pepper to taste

Directions:

1. Fill a pan with water and cook the cauliflower florets.
2. While the cauliflower is cooking, toss the cabbage, parmesan, basil, olives and garlic in a bowl.
3. Add the cooled cauliflower and season with salt and pepper.
4. Combine the vinegar and oil.
5. Drizzle the dressing over the salad.

Ingredients for Meatballs

- 1 lb. ground beef or turkey
- ⅓ cup feta cheese

- 1 tablespoon chopped sundried tomatoes
- ½ teaspoon thyme
- 1 large egg
- ¼ cup almond flour
- 1 tablespoon water
- 2 tablespoons oil

Directions:

1. Mix together the ingredients, (except for the olive oil). It's okay to use your fingers.
2. Shape the mixture into small meatballs.
3. Heat the olive oil in a skillet and fry the meatballs until they are brown and crispy.
4. Eat with the cauliflower salad.

Dinner

Slow Cooker Pot Roast

This pot roast is a snap to prepare in the slow cooker.

Ingredients:

- 1 3-lb. chuck roast
- 2 diced garlic cloves
- 1 chopped small onion
- 3 chopped celery stalks
- 3 chopped carrots
- 2 cups beef broth
- ½ cup red wine

Directions:

1. Salt and pepper the roast.
2. Brown the roast in a skillet.
3. Using a 4 or 5 quart slow cooker, place all ingredients inside the cooker.
4. Stir a bit to combine.
5. Cook for 6-7 hours on low.

Day 5

(Daily: 1445 calories, 102g fat, 15.5g net carbs, 76g protein)

Breakfast

Chocolate Smoothie

2 servings

Ingredients

- 1 ½ cup almond milk
- 1/2 peeled avocado
- ½ cup raspberries – can be frozen
- 1 tablespoon unsweetened cocoa powder
- 1 tablespoon stevia

Directions

1. Place the ingredients in a blender and pulse until smooth.

Lunch

2 servings

Pizza

Yes, you get to enjoy pizza!

Ingredients:

- 1 cup almond flour
- 2 tablespoon freshly grated parmesan cheese
- 2 tablespoon cream cheese
- ½ teaspoon salt
- 1 teaspoon oregano
- 1 large egg
- 1 ½ cups of shredded mozzarella
- 1 ½ cups homemade or bought pizza sauce

Directions:

1. Place the cheese in a large bowl and microwave for 30 seconds. It should be melted.
2. When the cheese has cooled a bit, add all of the other ingredients (except for the sauce) to the bowl.
3. Knead the dough with your fingers. Be sure to distribute the mozzarella evenly. The dough will be quite sticky.
4. Form the dough into a ball. Add almond flour if necessary.
5. Line a baking sheet with parchment paper and spray with Spam.
6. Flatten the dough with your fingers and place on the baking sheet.
7. Broil the pizza crust for 5-6 minutes. Keep it several inches from the heat.
8. After 5 minutes, remove the crust from the broiler. Using a fresh parchment liner, flip the crust over. The browned portion is now on the bottom.
9. Return to oven and bake until the dough is done, another 5 minutes.
10. Spread the pizza sauce over the top. Broil for 5 more minutes.

Dinner

Chicken with Gravy and Spinach

2 servings

Ingredients for Chicken:

- 4 chicken thighs with skin and bones
- 1 tablespoon paprika
- 1 teaspoon onion powder
- Salt and pepper to taste
- 1/3 cup sour cream

Directions:

1. Mix the spices in a bowl and rub on the chicken thighs.
2. Transfer the spiced thighs to a lined baking sheet.
3. Bake for 40 minutes at 400 degrees.
4. Collect the drippings and whisk together with the sour cream and use as gravy.
5. Serve with creamed spinach

Ingredients for Creamed Spinach:

- ¼ cup coconut milk
- 3 cups baby spinach
- 2 teaspoon Stevia
- A dash of nutmeg
- Salt and pepper to taste

Directions:

1. Wash the spinach thoroughly.
2. Warm the coconut milk in a pan and add in the spinach.
3. Stir until the spinach is wilted.
4. Adjust the seasoning.

Day 6

(Daily: 1838 calories, 143g fat, 18g net carbs, 80g protein)

Breakfast

Jalapeno & Cheesy Muffin with eggs and bacon

2 servings

Ingredients:

- 2 cups uncooked cauliflower
- 1 tablespoon of finely minced jalapeno
- 2 large, beaten eggs
- 2 tablespoon soft or melted butter
- ¼ cup grated parmesan
- 1 cup grated mozzarella
- ¾ cup grated cheddar
- 1 teaspoon onion flakes
- Salt and pepper to taste
- ½ teaspoon baking powder
- ¼ cup almond flour

Directions:

1. Press the cauliflower through a ricer.
2. Mix the cauliflower, eggs, jalapeno and butter in a medium bowl.
3. Add in all of the cheeses and combine well.
4. Add the seasoning, baking powder and flour. Mix thoroughly.

5. Butter the bottom of 12 muffin cups.
6. Fill the muffin cups with the batter.
7. Preheat the oven to 370 degrees and bake for about 30 minutes.
8. Turn the stove off, but leave the muffins for an hour. This will help them get firm.
9. Serve the muffins with eggs made to your liking and two slices of bacon.

Lunch

Taco Salad

2 servings

Ingredients:

- 1/2 lb. ground beef
- 2 tablespoons taco seasoning
- 5 cups romaine lettuce
- ½ cup chopped green peppers
- 1 sliced scallion
- ½ cup shredded cheddar cheese
- 1 sliced avocado
- 1 chopped tomato
- 4 tablespoons ranch dressing

Directions:

1. Cook the ground beef in a pan. Add the taco seasoning.
2. Shred the lettuce and add the avocado, bell peppers, scallions, tomato and cheese.
3. Top with the ground beef.

4. Add ranch dressing.

Dinner

Jalapeno Soup

4 servings

Ingredients:

- 3 cups chicken broth
- ½ cup milk or cream
- 2 cups diced onion
- 1 teaspoon garlic salt
- 1 lb. cubed cheddar cheese
- 1 cup diced jalapeno pepper
- 1/2 cup diced tomatoes

Directions:

1. Heat the broth, milk, onion, tomatoes and garlic salt in a pot.
2. Cook for about 10 minutes.
3. Remove pan from stove and add the cheese.
4. Puree the soup in a food processor to a smooth consistency.
5. Transfer the soup back to the pot and warm.
6. Add the jalapenos.
7. Serve the soup with a jalapenos muffin.

Day 7

(Daily: 1670 calories, 194g fat, 19.2g net carbs, 92g protein)

Breakfast

Blueberry Muffins

15 servings

Ingredients:

- 2 cups almond flour
- 1 cup heavy cream
- 2 large eggs
- 1/8 cup melted butter
- 6 tablespoons stevia
- ½ teaspoon baking soda
- ½ teaspoon lemon extract or lemon zest
- ¼ teaspoon salt
- ½ cup blueberries

Directions:

1. Preheat the oven to 350 degrees.
2. Place cupcake wrappers inside individual muffin cups
3. Combine the flour and the cream.
4. Add the eggs and mix thoroughly.
5. Mix in the melted butter, stevia, lemon extract, salt and baking soda.
6. Stir in the blueberries.
7. Fill 15 muffin cups till they are half filled with batter.
8. Bake for 20 minutes.

9. Allow the muffins to cool.
10. Serve them with butter.

Lunch

Fried calamari with a spicy aioli

1 serving

Ingredients:

- 4 oz. of squid, cleaned and sliced
- 1 large, beaten egg
- 3 tablespoons coconut flour
- 1/8 teaspoon paprika
- Salt and pepper to taste
- 1 cup coconut oil

Directions:

1. Set out 2 shallow bowls.
2. Fill one bowl with the beaten egg.
3. Fill the second bowl with the flour, paprika, salt and pepper.
4. Dredge the calamari slices through the egg.
5. Dredge the calamari slices through the spiced flour.
6. Heat the coconut oil in a deep frying.
7. Fry the calamari for 4-5 minutes until they are crispy brown.
8. While placing the calamari on paper towels to absorb the grease, prepare the aioli as follows:

Aioli Ingredients:

- 1 yolk
- 4 grated garlic cloves
- ½ teaspoon kosher salt
- 1/3 cup olive oil

Directions:

1. Whisk all ingredients except for the oil.
2. Slowly, drizzle in the olive oil while continuing to whisk.
3. The aioli should become stiff like mayonnaise.

Dinner

Steak with Crispy Brussel Sprouts

Ingredients for Brussels Sprouts:

4 servings

- ¼ cup coconut oil
- 16 oz. – 1 package – of bacon
- 20 Brussel sprouts – fresh is best.

Ingredients for Sauce:

- 3 tablespoons mayonnaise
- 1 tablespoon mustard
- ¼ teaspoon hot sauce
- 1 minced garlic clove
- Dash of salt
- Dash of liquid stevia

- 2 tablespoons capers

Directions:

1. Fry the bacon in a skillet.
2. Chop the cooked bacon into pieces and set aside.
3. Using another skillet, heat the coconut oil.
4. Fry the brussel sprouts well. Remove from skillet and blot with paper towel.
5. Transfer sprouts back into the skillet and fry again for 4 minutes. They need to be crunchy.
6. For the sauce, mix all ingredients except for the capers.
7. Place the blotted brussel sprouts in a bowl. Mix in the bacon bits and the capers.
8. Drizzle the brussel sprouts with the sauce.

Ingredients for Steak

- 1 T-Bone or other steak.
- 4 tablespoons butter
- Salt and pepper to taste

Directions:

1. Season the steak with the salt and pepper.
2. Let sit at room temperature for half an hour.
3. Heat the butter in a pan until it starts to smoke.
4. Transfer the steak to the pan. Fry for 90 seconds on each side.
5. This will result in a medium-rate steak. You can adjust to your own preference.

Day 8

(Daily: 1736 calories, 82g fat, 35g net carbs, 105g protein)

Breakfast

Ham & Cheese Casserole

4 servings

Ingredients for the crust:

- 4 cups peeled and shredded celery root (1 celery root)
- 3 tablespoons melted butter
- Salt and pepper to taste
- 2 tablespoon coconut flour
- 3 tablespoon parmesan cheese
- 1 ½ tablespoon olive oil

Ingredients for the Filling:

- 6 eggs
- 1 cup cream or half & half
- 1 cup almond milk
- ¾ cup baby spinach
- 2 cups diced ham
- 1 cup shredded cheddar cheese
- Salt and pepper to taste

Directions for the crust:

1. Preheat oven to 400 degrees.
2. Thoroughly combine all of the ingredients.
3. Use your fingers to press the crust into an 8 x 11 baking dish.
4. Bake for 20 minutes.
5. Set the crust aside.

Directions for the filling:

1. Lower the oven temperature to 350 degrees.
2. Combine the eggs, cream, milk, salt and pepper thoroughly.
3. Wash the spinach and add to the egg mixture.
4. Place the ham and cheese on top of the crust.
5. Pour the egg mixture over the ham and cheese.
6. Bake for 1 hour.
7. Allow to cool, then cut into slices.

Lunch

Pulled Pork with Stir-Fried Vegetables

Serving -10

Ingredients:

- 1 4-5 lb. pork shoulder
- ¼ teaspoon cumin
- ¼ teaspoon paprika
- ¼ teaspoon cinnamon
- Salt and pepper to taste

Directions:

1. Preheat the oven to 375 degrees.
2. With a sharp knife, make a few cuts through the fat of the pork shoulder.
3. Combine the spices for a rub.
4. Rub the spices over the entire pork shoulder.
5. Transfer the spiced shoulder to a large pot and roast for 30 minutes
6. Reduce the heat to 325 and roast for another 4 to5 hours.
7. Remove the pork shoulder from the oven.
8. When it is cool enough, pull the meat apart with 2 forks.
9. Serve with stir-fried vegetables.

Vegetable Stir Fry

Ingredients:

1 bag of frozen mixed vegetables.
6 slices bacon
2 tablespoons soy sauce
4 tablespoons olive oil

Directions:

1. Fry the bacon in a skillet.
2. Drain the bacon on a paper towel and cut into pieces. Set aside.
3. Heat the olive oil in a skillet or a wok. It should be hot.
4. Add the bacon and vegetables to the skillet.
5. Mix in the soy sauce and stir.
6. Keep stirring until the vegetables are done.
7. Serve with the pulled pork.

Dinner

Pizza Casserole

Ingredients:

- 4 cups of cauliflower florets
- 1 tablespoon butter
- 1 minced garlic clove
- 1 diced onion
- 1 tablespoon balsamic vinegar
- 1 cup heavy cream
- 4 tablespoons tomato paste
- 6 oz. cream cheese, cut into pieces
- 4 cups mozzarella cheese
- 2 teaspoons chopped basil
- Salt and pepper to taste
- 3 oz. sliced pepperoni
- Red pepper flakes – optional

Direction:

1. Preheat oven to 350 degrees.
2. Cook the cauliflower florets in a pan of water until they are just done. They should be a bit crisp, and not overdone. Set aside.
3. Heat the butter in a skillet.
4. Sauté the onion and garlic until they are aromatic and soft.
5. Add the vinegar. Deglaze the skillet and let simmer for 4-5 minutes.

6. Mix in the tomato paste and cream cheese. Keep stirring until the cream cheese melts and the consistency is smooth.
7. Add 2 cups of the mozzarella.
8. Let simmer and continue stirring until the ingredients are creamy and thick.
9. Add the basil, salt, pepper and red pepper flakes, if using.
10. Take the skillet off the stove.
11. Spray a baking dish with non-stick oil.
12. Line the bottom of the dish with half of the cauliflower and top with half of the pepperoni.
13. Add 1 cup of the mozzarella.
14. Create a second layer of cauliflower and pepperoni.
15. Spoon the cream cheese sauce over the entire dish and layer the remaining mozzarella on top.
16. Bake for 30 minutes. Take the casserole out and let sit for a few minutes.

Day 9

(Daily: 1045 calories, 42g fat, 16.37g net carbs, 58g protein)

Breakfast

Breakfast Casserole

12 serving

Ingredients:

- 1 dozen large eggs
- 1/3 cup whipping cream
- 1 cup ricotta cheese
- 1 diced onion
- Salt and pepper to taste
- 1 teaspoon Italian seasoning
- 1 package frozen spinach, thawed.
- 1 lb. sliced ham

Directions:

1. Preheat oven to 350 degrees.
2. Take 4 eggs, cream, onion and ricotta cheese and whip until nice and smooth.
3. Use a second bowl to whip the remaining eggs.
4. Add the first eggy cheese mix to the whipped eggs and blend thoroughly.
5. Mix in the salt, pepper and Italian seasoning.
6. Add the spinach.
7. Spray a baking dish with non-stick oil.

8. Layer the bottom with the ham and pour in the casserole mixture.
9. Bake for 30 minutes.

Lunch

Kale and Sausage Soup

6 servings

Directions:

- 1 lb. non-spicy Italian sausage
- 1 tablespoon butter
- 1 chopped onion
- 2 peeled and cut carrots
- 1 minced garlic clove
- 2 tablespoon balsamic vinegar
- 1 teaspoon basil
- 1 teaspoon oregano
- ¼ tablespoon red pepper flakes
- 4 cups chicken broth
- ½ cup half & half or heavy cream
- 2 cups cauliflower florets
- 2 cups cut-up kale
- Salt and pepper to taste

Directions:

1. Sauté the sausage meat in a large pan or Dutch oven until meat is brown.
2. Transfer the sausage to plate with a slotted spoon.

3. Use a paper towel to drain the fat from the sausage. Discard any remaining fat in the pan, but don't clean the pan.
4. In the same pan, sauté the onion and carrots with the butter.
5. Add the garlic and stir a bit, then drizzle in the balsamic vinegar. Cook for a minute.
6. Stir in the spices, the chicken stock, and then the cream.
7. Let the soup simmer for a minute.
8. Add in the cauliflower florets and simmer for 10 minutes.
9. Mix in the sausage meat and kale and cook for another minute.
10. Adjust the seasoning and enjoy.

Dinner

Chicken Pad Thai

2 servings

Ingredients:

- 1 tablespoon olive oil
- 1 chopped onion
- 2 diced garlic cloves
- 4 chicken thighs, skinless and boneless
- Salt and pepper to taste
- 1 chopped zucchini
- 1 egg
- 2 tablespoon soy sauce
- Juice of 1 lime
- 1 tablespoon peanuts

Directions:

1. Heat the oil in a skillet or wok and sauté the onion for 5 minutes.
2. Add the garlic and continue sautéing for 2-3 minutes.
3. Season the chicken thighs and transfer them to the skillet.
4. Cook on both sides until the chicken is done.
5. Place the chicken on a plate and use two forks to shred the meat.
6. Break the egg in the middle of the skillet or wok. Use a spatula to lightly scramble it.
7. Add the zucchini pieces and stir into the scrambled egg for a minute or so.
8. Mix in the shredded chicken and drizzle with the lime juice and soy sauce.
9. Place the Pad Tai on a plate and top with chopped peanuts.
10. Adjust seasoning if necessary.

Day 10

Daily: 1277 calories, 98g fat, 12g net carbs, 58g protein)

Breakfast

Scotch Eggs

1 serving

Ingredients:

- 2 eggs
- 4 oz. breakfast sausage
- Salt and pepper to taste
- Avocado slices

Directions:

1. Line 2 muffin cups with the sausage meat (simply press down with your fingers.).
2. Bake for 8 minutes at 350 degrees.
3. Take muffins out of oven and crack 1 egg into each.
4. Return cups to oven and bake for another 10-12 minutes, a few minutes longer for a fully done yolk.
5. Season with salt and pepper.
6. Serve with avocado slices and hot sauce, if desired.

Lunch

Egg Salad on Lettuce with Bacon

1 serving

Ingredients for Egg Salad:

- 2 eggs
- 2 teaspoon mayonnaise without sugar
- ¼ teaspoon mustard
- 2 drops of lemon juice
- Dash of salt and pepper

Directions:

1. Bring a pan of water to boil and cook the eggs for 10 minutes.
2. Let the eggs cool before peeling.
3. Chop the eggs manually or use a food processor.
4. Mix in all the other ingredients and blend well.
5. Fry 2 slices of bacon.
6. Place a few romaine lettuce leaves on a plate and top with the egg salad and the bacon slices.

Dinner

Fake Falafel with Sauce

2 servings of 2 patties each

Ingredients for Fake Falafel:

- 1 cup uncooked cauliflower
- ¼ cup almonds
- ¼ tablespoon coriander
- ¼ teaspoon salt
- Dash of cayenne pepper
- ½ minced garlic clove
- 1 tablespoon chopped parsley
- 1 egg
- 2 tablespoons coconut flour
- 3 tablespoons olive oil

Ingredients for Sauce:

- 1 tablespoon tahini paste
- 2 tablespoon water
- 1 teaspoon lemon juice
- ½ minced garlic clove
- Dash of salt

Directions:

1. Chop up a cauliflower and pulse the florets in a food processor until they reach a grainy consistency.
2. Grind the almonds, but leave a bit of texture.
3. Toss the cauliflower and almonds in a bowl and add the remaining ingredients.
4. Stir until all ingredients are combined.
5. Heat the olive oil in a pan.
6. While the oil is heating, form 4 patties with the falafel mixture.
7. Fry the patties until golden brown.

8. For the sauce, combine the ingredients and blend well.
9. Drizzle the sauce over the patties.
10. Serve with tomato slices.

Day 11

(Totals: 1210 calories, 125g fat, 12.5g net carbs, 72g protein)

Breakfast

2 servings

Sweet Pancakes

Ingredients:

- 2 eggs
- 2 oz. softened cream cheese
- 1 tablespoons almond flour
- ½ teaspoon cinnamon
- 2 teaspoon stevia
- 1/8 teaspoon salt
- 1/4 cup shredded coconut
- 1 tablespoon butter
- Sugar-free maple syrup

Directions:

1. Whisk the eggs fluffy in a bowl.
2. Mix in the cream cheese and thoroughly blend.
3. Add the flour, stevia, cinnamon and salt.
4. Melt the butter in a skillet and pour in half of the batter.
5. Cook for 4-5 minutes, then flip the pancake to the other side.
6. Repeat with the remaining batter.
7. Top the pancakes with the shredded coconuts and drizzle with the syrup.

Lunch

Greek Lemon Soup with Muffin

4 servings

Ingredients:

- 4 cups chicken broth
- 3 large eggs
- 1/3 cup lemon juice
- 2 cups cauliflower florets
- 2 cups cooked chicken
- Salt and pepper to taste
- Lemon slices for garnish

Directions:

1. Put the cauliflower florets in a food processor and pulse until the cauliflower is the size and consistency of rice. Set aside.
2. Shred the chicken using 2 forks.
3. Heat the broth in a saucepan.
4. In a bowl, whip up the eggs and add the lemon juice.
5. Pour 1 cup of the heated broth into the egg mix. Keep stirring until well-blended.
6. Transfer the broth/egg mixture into the pan with the remaining broth.
7. Transfer 1 cup of the processed cauliflower and ½ cup chicken.
8. Add about 1 cup of the cauliflower rice and ½ cup of shredded chicken to a blender and puree.
9. Return the pureed rice and chicken to the pan.

10. Add the remaining chicken and cauliflower, stir, and simmer for 7-8 minutes.
11. Season to taste.
12. Garnish a bowl with the lemon slices and serve hot.
13. You should have a few jalapeno cheddar muffins in the freezer. While preparing the soup, thaw the muffin and heat for a few minutes in the oven.

Dinner

Tandoori Chicken with Spinach

2 servings

Ingredients:

- 2 lbs. chicken legs

Marinade #1:

- 2 teaspoon minced garlic
- 1 teaspoon grated ginger
- 1 teaspoon Kashmiri chili powder
- 1 teaspoon salt
- 2 teaspoon lemon juice
- 3 teaspoons olive oil

Marinade #2

- 1/4 cup yogurt
- 2 teaspoon garlic powder
- 1 teaspoon grated ginger
- 1 teaspoon allspice
- 1 teaspoon Kashmiri chili powder

- 1 teaspoon salt
- 1/2 teaspoon cinnamon
- 1/2 teaspoon cumin
- 1/2 teaspoon Garam Masala
- 2 teaspoon lemon juice

Directions:

1. Use a sharp knife to cut several slits in the chicken legs.
2. Blend the first marinade ingredients together and rub into the chicken meat.
3. Refrigerate for at least an hour.
4. Blend the second marinade ingredients together and thoroughly dredge the chicken legs.
5. Preheat the oven to 375 degrees.
6. Line a baking dish with foil or parchment and place the chicken legs on top.
7. Bake for about 35 minutes or until the chicken is crispy.
8. Serve with creamed spinach

Creamed Spinach

2 servings

Ingredients:

- 4 cups baby spinach
- ¼ cup coconut milk
- Dash of nutmeg
- 2 teaspoon stevia
- Salt and pepper to taste

Directions:

1. Thoroughly wash the spinach.
2. In a pan, warm up the coconut milk.
3. Stir in the spinach and simmer until the spinach is wilted. Keep stirring.
4. Adjust seasoning and serve with the chicken.

Day 12

Daily: 1570 calories, 116g fat, 11g carbs, 98g protein)

Breakfast

Monte Cristo Bake with Poached Egg

Ingredients:

- 4 cream cheese pancakes – see Day 4
- 4 slices Canadian bacon
- 2 cups shredded Swiss cheese
- Sugar-free syrup

Directions:

1. Preheat oven to375 degrees.
2. Butter a baking dish and cover the bottom with 2 of the cream cheese pancakes.
3. Top the pancakes with 2 slices of Canadian bacon and 1 cup Swiss cheese.
4. Repeat the layering.
5. Bake for 15 minutes.
6. Transfer to a platter and drizzle with sugar-free syrup and a poached egg*.

Note: *The best way to poach an egg is to bring a pan of water to boil, crack the egg into the boiling water, and then take the pan off the burner.

Lunch

BBQ Ribs with Slaw

Ingredients for Ribs:

- 3 lbs. baby back ribs
- 1 cup jerk seasoning

Ingredients for Sauce:

- ¼ cup gluten free soy sauce
- ¼ cup water
- 3 tablespoons grated ginger
- 1 tablespoon orange zest
- ¼ cup fresh orange juice
- 2 tablespoons cider vinegar
- 4 tablespoons white vinegar
- 1 tablespoon Worcestershire sauce or steak sauce
- 1 tablespoon mustard
- 2 tablespoons stevia
- 1 teaspoon coconut flour

Directions:

1. Preheat oven to 325 degrees.
2. Rub the jerk seasoning into the ribs and coat thoroughly.
3. Place ribs on a baking sheet and bake for 3 hours.
4. While ribs are cooking, prepare the sauce.
5. Stir together all of the sauce ingredients in a pan.
6. As soon as the liquid starts to boil, lower the heat and simmer for 10 minutes.
7. Pour the sauce through a sieve and toss the orange zest.

8. Return the sauce to the pan and stir in the coconut flour to thicken.
9. Cook for 5 minutes.
10. Spoon the sauce over the ribs and bake for 30 minutes at 370 degrees.
11. Serve with the broccoli slaw.

Broccoli Slaw

Ingredients:

- 2 tablespoon olive oil
- ¼ cup mayonnaise without sugar
- 2 tablespoon cider vinegar
- 1 tablespoon Dijon mustard
- 2 tablespoon stevia
- Salt and pepper to taste
- ½ cup golden raisins
- 1 bag broccoli slaw

Directions:

1. Mix together all of the ingredients except the raisins and the slaw.
2. Toss the slaw and raisings in a bowl and top with the dressing.
3. Serve with the BBQ ribs.

Dinner

Fried Chicken with Spinach Salad

Ingredients for Fried Chicken:

6 servings

- 5 lbs. chicken legs
- 1 teaspoon each salt, pepper paprika and garlic powder
- 1 cup almond flour
- ½ cup oil to fry the chicken

Directions:

1. Combine all of the spices and seasoning and coat the chicken.
2. Refrigerate the chicken for 4 hours or overnight.
3. Dredge the chicken through the flour.
4. Heat the oil in a skillet.
5. Fry the chicken in batches until nice and brown, about 8-10 minutes per side.

Spinach Salad

6 servings

Ingredients:

- 6 cups baby spinach
- 1 cup diced red onion

- ¼ cup blue cheese
- ½ cup almond slivers
- 1 cup cooked bacon pieces

Directions:

1. Wash the spinach and place in a large bowl.
2. Add the remaining ingredients and toss.
3. Drizzle a low carb dressing over the salad and serve.

Day 13

Daily: 1449 calories, 111g fat, 19g carbs, 89g protein)

Breakfast

Breakfast Smoothie

Ingredients:

- 2 cups almond milk
- 1 oz. spinach or kale
- ½ cup diced cucumber
- ½ cup diced celery
- 1 diced avocado
- 2 tablespoons coconut oil
- 2 tablespoons liquid stevia
- ¼ cup protein powder

Directions:

1. Place the almond milk and spinach in a blender and puree for a second or two.
2. Add all remaining ingredients and puree until smooth and creamy.

Lunch

Stuffed Zucchini

2 servings

Ingredients:

- 2 large zucchinis
- 2 tablespoons melted butter
- 4 oz. shredded cheddar cheese
- 1 cup chopped broccoli
- 1 ½ cups shredded cooked chicken
- 3 tablespoons sour cream
- 3 tablespoons diced scallion
- Salt and Pepper to taste

Directions:

1. Preheat oven to 400 degrees.
2. Cut zucchinis in half lengthwise.
3. Remove most of the inner zucchini meat. You want a half-inch thick shell.
4. Drizzle the melted butter into both zucchini shells. Add salt and pepper and cook for 20 minutes.
5. In a bowl, mix the shredded chicken, chopped broccoli and sour cream. Add salt and pepper if desired.
6. Remove the zucchini shells from the oven and stuff with the chicken mixture.
7. Top with the shredded cheese.
8. Bake for another 10 minutes.
9. Sprinkle with chopped scallions and enjoy.

Dinner

Tuna Salad

1 serving

Ingredients:

- 2 cups mixed greens
- 1 diced tomato
- ¼ cup chopped parsley
- 2 oz. chopped mint
- ½ cup pitted kalamata olives
- 1 diced avocado
- 1 chopped scallion
- 1 can albacore tuna
- 2 tablespoons olive oil
- 1 tablespoon cider vinegar
- Salt and pepper to taste

Directions:

1. Using a fork, flake the tuna into small pieces.
2. Toss all ingredients in a large bowl and toss until combined.

Day 14

Steak and Eggs

Daily: 1875 calories, 98g fat, 18g carbs, 97g protein)

1 serving

Ingredients:

- 1 tablespoon butter
- 2 large eggs
- 4 oz. sirloin steak
- 3 avocado slices (have the rest as a mid-morning snack)
- Salt and pepper to taste

Directions:

1. Fry the eggs in the melted butter.
2. Using another skillet, fry the steak to favorite doneness. Slice the steak in pieces and top with the fried eggs.
3. Season with the salt and pepper.
4. Serve with the avocado slices.

Lunch

Fish Bake

6 servings

Ingredients:

- 4 eggs
- 1 cauliflower
- ½ cup butter
- 10 oz. firm white fish such as cod
- 10 oz. salmon fillets
- 1 diced onion
- 1 bay leaf
- 3 cloves
- 1 cup whipping cream
- 1 teaspoon Dijon mustard
- 1 ½ cup shredded cheddar cheese
- 3 tablespoons chopped chives
- Salt and pepper to taste

Directions:

1. Bring a saucepan of water to boil and add salt.
2. Boil the eggs for 10 minutes.
3. Chop the cauliflower into florets. Either stream or boil them until just done. You don't want them soft and soggy.
4. Transfer the florets to a food processor and add ¼ cup of butter. Process to a creamy consistency. Set aside.
5. Remove skin from all of the fish and chop into bite-sized pieces.
6. Put the fish in a dish and cover with the cream and ½ cup of water.
7. Add the onions and seasoning.
8. Bring the liquid to a boil on the stove and simmer for 10 minutes.
9. Add the rest of the butter.
10. Toss the cloves and bay leaf.
11. Stir in 1 cup of the cheese. Let the cheese melt.

12. Cut the eggs and layer on top of the fish.
13. Add the chives and the creamed cauliflower.
14. Top with remaining cheese.
15. Bake for 30 minutes.

Dinner

Curried Lamb

4 servings

Ingredients:

- 2 lbs. lamb meat
- 1 diced onion
- 2 diced garlic cloves
- 1 chopped tomato
- 14 oz. coconut milk
- ½ teaspoon ginger
- ½ teaspoon ginger
- ½ teaspoon cumin
- 1 teaspoon garam masala
- 3 tablespoons coconut oil

Directions:

1. Cut the lamb into bite-sized chunks.
2. Sauté the tomato and onion in the coconut oil for 5 minutes.
3. Stir in the garlic and all of the spices. Cook for another 5 minutes.
4. Add the lamb until the meat has browned.
5. Pour in the coconut milk and let the milk boil.
6. Lower the heat to a simmer and cook for 50 minutes.

Day 15

(Daily: 1258 calories, 60g fat, 14g carbs, 37g protein)

Breakfast

1 serving

Cereal

Ingredients:

- 1/4 cup slivered almonds
- 3 tablespoons crushed pecans
- 3 tablespoons flaxseeds
- 1 tablespoon chia seeds
- 1 tablespoon shredded coconut
- 1 small sliced banana or 2 sliced strawberries
- Dash of stevia
- ¼ cup almond or coconut milk

Directions:

1. Combine all ingredients except for the stevia and milk.
2. Add a pinch of stevia for sweetness and enjoy with some low carb milk.

Lunch

Italian Meatballs

1 serving – 6 meatballs

Ingredients:

- 1 diced onion
- 2 tablespoon olive oil
- 1 cup ricotta cheese
- 1 egg
- 1 diced garlic clove
- 1 teaspoons Italian seasoning
- Salt and pepper to taste
- 3/4 cup shredded asiago cheese
- ½ lb. ground beef
- ½ lb. Italian sausage

Directions:

1. Preheat oven to 350 degrees.
2. Sauté the onions for 10 minutes in the olive oil. Set aside.
3. Place the cheese in a food processor and pulse until it is grainy.
4. Combine the egg with the ricotta cheese. It should be rich and smooth.
5. Mix in the seasonings.
6. Mix in the onions and the cheese and combine thoroughly.
7. Mix in the beef and combine.
8. Form approximately 30 meatballs.
9. Transfer the meatballs to baking sheet.
10. Bake for 20 minutes.

11. Heat up some tomato sauce as a dip.

Dinner

Spicy Shrimp Soup

Serves: 6 servings

Ingredients:

- 2 lbs. peeled and deveined raw shrimp
- ¼ cup olive oil
- ¼ cup diced onion
- 1 minced garlic clove
- ¼ cup diced jalapeno peppers
- 6 tablespoons chopped cilantro
- 1 small can diced tomatoes
- 1 cup coconut milk
- 2 tablespoons hot sauce
- 1 tablespoon lime juice
- Salt and pepper to taste

Directions:

1. Heat the oil in a skillet and sauté the onions for about 5 minutes.
2. Stir in the pepper and garlic and sauté for another 5 minutes.
3. Mix in shrimp, tomatoes and cilantro and let simmer for 5 minutes.
4. Pour in the milk and hot sauce and bring to boil.
5. Immediate lower the heat and add the lime juice, salt and pepper.

ⅉ

(Daily: 1810 calories, 71g fat, 21g carbs, 62g protein)

Breakfast

Stuffed Crepes

1 serving

Ingredients for Crepes:

- 2 oz. cream cheese
- 2 large eggs
- 2 tablespoons butter
- 2 tablespoons stevia
- Dash of salt and cinnamon

Ingredients for Filling:

- ½ cup ricotta cheese
- 4 oz. raspberries (can be frozen or fresh)

Directions:

1. Put the batter ingredients in a food processor and puree until the cream cheese is creamy and smooth.
2. Melt the butter in a pan and add a quarter of the batter. The batter should be very thin.
3. Cook for a minute, then flip, and cook for 20 more seconds.
4. Repeat with the remaining batter. You should end up with 2 crepes per serving.

5. Spoon the cream cheese and raspberries down the center of each crepe.
6. Gently fold each crepe in half.
7. If desired, serve with whipped cream or sugar-free syrup.

Lunch

Buffalo Wings

1 serving

Ingredients:

- 6 chicken wings
- ¼ cup hot sauce
- 2 tablespoons butter
- Salt and pepper to taste
- ¼ teaspoon garlic powder
- ¼ teaspoon paprika

Directions:

1. Cut the tips off the wings.
2. Place the wings in a bowl and cover with hot sauce.
3. Refrigerate for at least 1 hour.
4. Mix the spices in a bowl and coat the wings.
5. Turn on the broiler.
6. Spray a baking sheet with non-stick spray.
7. Place the wings on the baking sheet.
8. Broil for 8 minutes.
9. While the wings are broiling, mix ¼ cup hot sauce with 3 tablespoons of butter in a small pan. For added heat, you can add some cayenne pepper. Stir until the butter is melted, then remove from stove.

10. Carefully remove the baking sheet from the broiler and turn the wings around.
11. Broil for an additional 6 minutes.
12. Serve the wings covered in the sauce or serve the sauce separately.
13. Serve the wings with some broccoli slaw.

Dinner

Seafood Gumbo

6 servings

Ingredients:

- 12 oz. sliced spicy chicken sausage
- 3 tablespoons olive oil
- 1 chopped bell pepper
- 1 cup chopped onions
- 2 minced garlic cloves
- 3 cups chicken broth
- 1 cup crushed tomatoes
- ¼ teaspoon cayenne pepper
- Salt and pepper to taste
- 1 bay leaf
- 1 lb. peeled and deveined shrimp
- 6 large scallops
- 1 can lump crabmeat
- 1 tablespoon chopped parsley

Directions:

1. In a large pot, heat the sausage slices until they are browned.
2. Drain the sausage on a paper towel.
3. In the same pot and with low heat, sauté the peppers, onions and garlic for 10 minutes.
4. Pour in the broth and stir in the seasonings and crushed tomatoes.
5. Let the broth boil, then simmer for 30-40 minutes.
6. Add the scallops and shrimps and continue to simmer for 5 minutes.
7. Add the sausage and crabmeat and stir.
8. Use the parsley to garnish the gumbo.

Day 17

(Daily: 1587 calories, 96.8g fat, 7.8g carbs, 71g protein)

Breakfast

Egg McMuffin

1 serving:

Ingredients:

- 1 large egg
- 1 tablespoon coconut milk
- 1 tablespoon coconut flour
- 1 teaspoon olive oil
- 1/2 teaspoon baking powder
- Dash of salt

Sandwich Filling

- 1 large egg
- 1 slice cheddar cheese
- 1 sausage patty
- Salt and pepper to taste
- 1/4 teaspoon sage

Directions:

1. Preheat the oven to 400 degrees.
2. Mix all the ingredients for the muffin in a bowl. Make sure there are no lumps.

3. Transfer the muffin batter to a ramekin and bake for about 15 minutes.
4. Fry the egg and the sausage patty. Season to taste.
5. Remove the muffin from the ramekin and cut it in half.
6. Toast the muffin halves.
7. Assemble your McMuffin by placing the fried egg and sausage on top of 1 muffin half and topping with the second half.

Lunch

Chicken Casserole

6 servings

Ingredients:

- 1 tablespoon olive oil
- 2 chicken breasts
- 1 cup sliced mushrooms
- ¼ cup mayonnaise
- 2 ½ cups cauliflower florets
- 1/3 cup heavy cream
- ½ cup chicken stock
- 1/2 cup low carb tomato sauce
- Salt and pepper to taste
- ¼ teaspoon garlic powder
- 1 cup shredded mozzarella cheese
- 3 tablespoons grated parmesan cheese

Directions:

1. Preheat the oven to 375 degrees
2. Use a grater to rice the cauliflower.

3. Cook the cauliflower in the broth for 15 minutes. The broth should be evaporated.
4. Pour in the heavy cream and continue to cook the cauliflower for 5 minutes.
5. Heat the olive oil and cook the chicken.
6. When the chicken is done, use 2 forks to shred the meat.
7. Add the mushrooms to the chicken.
8. Mix in the mayonnaise and combine well.
9. Stir in the cauliflower and seasonings and mix.
10. Add the tomato sauce.
11. Transfer the casserole to a baking dish.
12. Top with the cheeses.
13. Bake the casserole for 20 minutes.

Dinner

Caesar Salad

4 servings

Ingredients:

- 1 egg yolk
- 8 tablespoons olive oil
- 4 tablespoons lemon juice
- 1 teaspoon Dijon mustard
- 6 anchovy filets
- 2 diced cloves of garlic
- 6 tablespoons grated parmesan cheese
- shredded romaine lettuce leaves.

Directions:

1. In a blender, mix together the egg yolk and mustard.
2. Pour in the olive oil and continue blending.
3. Add in the anchovies, lemon juice, 4 tablespoons of parmesan cheese and the garlic.
4. Blend until the dressing is smooth.
5. Arrange the romaine lettuce on plates.
6. Top with the dressing and remaining parmesan cheese.
7. If desired, use pork rinds as croutons.

Day 18

(Daily: 1144 calories, 68.9g fat, 32.9g carbs, 32.9g protein)

Breakfast

Feta Omelet

1 serving

Ingredients:

- 1 tablespoon butter
- 3 large eggs
- 1 tablespoon half & half
- 2 tablespoons feta cheese
- 1 tablespoon pesto
- Salt and pepper to taste

Directions:

1. Heat the butter in a skillet.
2. Whip the eggs and half & half in a small bowl.
3. When the butter is hot, pour the eggs into the skillet.
4. When the omelet is almost done, spoon the feta cheese and pesto onto one half, then fold it over the other half.
5. Cook for 3-4 more minutes.
6. If desired, sprinkle some feta cheese on top before serving.

Lunch

Eggplant Roulade

4 servings

Ingredients:

- 2 eggplants
- 1 cups shredded mozzarella
- 1 cup ricotta cheese
- 1/2 cup shredded parmesan
- 9 oz. frozen spinach with the liquid squeezed out.
- 1 large egg
- 1 minced garlic clove
- Salt and pepper to taste
- 1 cup tomato marinara
- 1 extra cup shredded mozzarella

Directions:

1. Preheat the oven to 350 degrees.
2. Peal the eggplants and thinly slice them lengthwise.
3. Lightly grease a baking sheet and place the slices on the sheet.
4. Cook for 10 minutes. Set aside.
5. Combine the spinach, egg, the 3 cheeses and garlic. Add the salt and pepper
6. Pour 1/2 cup of the tomato sauce onto a baking dish.
7. Heap 2 tablespoons of the spinach/cheese mix onto each eggplant slice.
8. Roll up all the slices and fastened with toothpicks.
9. Place the eggplant roulade onto the tomato sauce in the baking sheet.

10. Top with the rest of the sauce and the additional mozzarella.
11. Bake for 35 – 40 minutes.

Dinner

Liver and Onions

2 servings

Ingredients:

- ½ lb. bacon
- 2 lbs. beef liver
- 1 sliced onion
- 2 diced garlic cloves
- ½ cup of sliced mushrooms
- Salt and pepper to taste

Directions:

1. Fry the bacon, onion and garlic.
2. Stir in the mushrooms and seasoning.
3. Transfer these ingredients to a plate and cook the liver in the same skillet, about 2 minutes both sides.
4. Add the bacon mix to the liver and cook for abouy7-8 minutes.

Day 19

(Daily: 2156 calories, 126.1g fat, 21.6g carbs, 167.3g protein)

Breakfast

Eggs Benedict

2 servings

Ingredients:

- 4 rolls
- 4 large eggs
- 4 slices Canadian bacon
- 2 tablespoons white vinegar
- 1 ½ teaspoon chives

Ingredients for hollandaise sauce

- 2 egg yolks
- 2 tablespoons butter
- 1 teaspoon lemon juice
- Dash of salt

Ingredients for rolls:

- 12 servings (freeze them and have them as a snack.)
- 3 large eggs
- 4 oz. cream cheese
- 1/8 teaspoon cream of tartar
- Pinch of salt

Directions for rolls:

1. Preheat oven to 300 degrees.
2. Separate the eggs and place and yolks and white in separate bowls.
3. Whip the egg whites with a hand mixer until peaks form.
4. Mix in the cream of tartar and continue whipping.
5. Using the hand mixer, beat the yolks, the cream cheese and the salt until the mixture is creamy.
6. Gently fold egg whites into the yolk mixture.
7. Spray a baking sheet with non-stick oil.
8. Spoon the batter onto the baking sheet.
9. Bake for 40 minutes and allow the rolls to cool.

Directions for hollandaise sauce:

1. Whisk 3 egg yolks and add the lemon juice in a glass bowl.
2. In a sauce pan, melt the butter.
3. Fill a pan with a cup of water and bring to boil. Lower the heat to a simmer.
4. Set the glass bowl on top of the pan.
5. Keep whisking the egg yolks.
6. While continuing to whisk, drizzle in the melted butter.
7. When the hollandaise sauce is thick enough, remove from stove and add the salt. Then set aside.

Directions for Egg Benedict:

1. Poach 4 eggs in a pan of boiling water for 4 minutes.
2. Use a spatula to move the eggs to a plate.
3. Heat the Canadian bacon in a skillet for a minute or two.
4. Lay out 4 roll halves and top with a poached egg and a slice of Canadian bacon.

5. Drizzle hollandaise sauce over each egg and season with salt, pepper and a dash of chives.

Lunch

Spicy Chicken

4 servings

Ingredients:

- 2 tablespoons olive oil
- 2 lbs. chicken thighs
- 2 diced tomatoes
- 1 cup chicken stock
- 1 can coconut milk
- 2 teaspoons lime juice

Spice Rub:

- 3 diced green chilies
- 3 diced garlic cloves
- 1 cup chopped onion
- 2 tablespoons toasted peanuts
- 2 tablespoons grated ginger
- 1 tablespoon coriander
- 1 tablespoon cumin
- 1/2 teaspoon pepper
- ½ tablespoon water

Directions:

1. Make the spice rub by combining all ingredients in a blender to create a paste.

2. Cut the chicken into bite-sized pieces.
3. Heat the olive oil in a skillet and add the spice rub. Cook for about minutes while stirring.
4. Mix in the chicken pieces and continue cooking for 3 minutes.
5. Add in the stock and tomatoes and mix well.
6. Let the stock simmer at a low heat for 30 minutes.
7. Stir in the coconut milk and let cook for 20 more minutes
8. Turn off the heat and mix in the lime juice, salt and pepper.

Dinner

Steak with Wine Sauce

2 servings

Ingredients:

- 2 steaks
- 2 cups sliced mushrooms
- 4 oz. heavy cream
- ¼ cup wine
- 2 tablespoons butter
- Salt and Pepper to taste

Directions:

1. Preheat oven to 450 degrees.
2. Season the steaks on both sides.
3. Melt the butter in a cast iron skillet
4. When the butter starts to sizzle, sear the steaks on each side for about 2 minutes.

5. Carefully, using potholders, place the skillet in the oven.
6. Depending on the desired wellness, cook for 10 – 14 minutes, turning the steaks once during that time.
7. Place the steaks on a platter and cover lightly.
8. Use the wine to deglaze the skillet.
9. Mix in the cream and mushrooms and simmer a few minutes until the sauce is thickened.
10. Drizzle the sauce over the meat.
11. Serve with a steamed vegetable or chopped romaine lettuce and Ranch dressing.

Day 20

(Daily: 1082 calories, 50.9g fat, 21g carbs, 107g protein)

Breakfast

Cheddar Biscuits

2 biscuits are 1 serving. Freeze the rest for future use.

Ingredients:

- 2 ½ cups almond flour
- 6 ounces shredded cheddar cheese
- 5 tablespoons butter
- 8 oz. cream cheese
- 3 eggs
- 2 teaspoons finely minced garlic
- 1 teaspoon baking soda
- 1 teaspoon xanthum gum
- ½ teaspoon salt

Directions:

1. Preheat oven to 325 degrees.
2. Cover a baking sheet with parchment paper.
3. Place 1 cup of the almond flour and the cheddar cheese in a food processor. Pulse until the ingredients are finely grained.
4. Place the cream cheese and the butter in a bowl and microwave for 20 seconds.

5. Remove from microwave and beat until creamy and smooth.
6. Beat in the eggs, garlic, salt and xanthum gum.
7. Mix in the almond flour/cheddar mixture as well as the remaining flour.
8. Keep mixing until you have a dough.
9. Use a spoon to drop the dough onto the cookie sheet.
10. Bake for 25 minutes. The biscuits should be a nice brown.
11. Let the biscuits cool for a few minutes.

Lunch

Spicy Fish Tacos

2 servings

Ingredients:

- 2 tablespoon olive oil
- 1 chopped jalapeno
- 1/2 diced onion
- 2 chipotle peppers in adobo sauce
- 2 minced garlic cloves
- 3 tablespoons butter
- 2 tablespoons mayonnaise
- 1 lb. cod fillets
- 4 low-carb tortillas

Directions:

1. Heat the oil in a skillet and sauté the onion until soft.
2. Lower the heat and mix in the garlic and jalapeño and stir for 2-3 minutes.

3. Dice the chipotles peppers. Stir the chipotle and sauce into the skillet.
4. Cut the cod into small pieces.
5. Add the cod, butter and mayo to the skillet.
6. Let cook for 8 minutes, stirring occasionally.
7. Heat the tortillas in another skillet, 2 minutes per side.
8. Fill the tortillas with the fish.

Dinner

Coconut Shrimp

Servings 2

Ingredients:

- 14 medium shrimp
- 1 large egg
- 1 cup shredded coconut
- ½ cup coconut flour
- 1 tablespoons lime juice
- ¼ teaspoon ground cumin
- ¼ teaspoon cayenne pepper
- ¼ teaspoon chili powder
- ¼ teaspoon paprika
- 2 diced garlic cloves
- Salt and pepper to taste
- Olive oil for frying

Directions:

1. Remove the shells and devein the shrimp, but leave the tails.
2. Drizzle the shrimp with lime juice.

3. Mix the cumin, cayenne pepper, chili powder, salt and pepper together.
4. Season the shrimp and place in refrigerator for an hour.
5. Whisk the egg in a shallow bowl.
6. Mix the coconut flour with the paprika and place in another shallow bowl.
7. Dredge each shrimp first through the flour mix, then through the egg.
8. Heat the olive oil in a large pan and sauté the garlic.
9. Fry the shrimp for 3 minutes on one side, then another 3 minutes on the other.
10. Have your favorite dipping sauce at the table.
11. Serve with Roasted Pecan Green Beans.

Day 21

(Daily: 1227 calories, 96g fat, 12g carbs, 76g protein)

Breakfast

Cheese Quiche

6 servings

Ingredients:

- 6 cups of shredded cheese such as cheddar, Colby jack or Muenster or any combination.
- 3 tablespoons butter
- 1 chopped onion
- 12 large eggs
- 2 cups whipping cream
- 1 teaspoon thyme
- Salt and pepper to taste.

Directions:

1. Preheat the oven to 350 degrees.
2. Melt the butter in a skillet and sauté the onions for 5 minutes. Set aside.
3. Spray 2 quiche pans with non-stick oil.
4. Place 1 cup of the cheese in each of the pans; top with half of the sautéed onions.
5. Whisk the eggs and cream in a large bowl. Add the thyme, salt and pepper.
6. Divide the eggs into the 2 pans.
7. Top with the remaining cheese and onions.

8. Bake for 25 minutes.
9. Serve and freeze the leftovers.

Note: You can add other vegetables and/or meats, if you desire.

Lunch

Meatloaf

12 servings

Ingredients:

- ¼ cup almond flour
- ¼ cup grated Parmesan cheese
- 1 tablespoon butter
- 2 tablespoons diced onion
- ½ cup diced green pepper
- 2 minced garlic cloves
- 1 large egg
- ½ tablespoon basil and thyme
- 2 tablespoons chopped parsley
- Salt and pepper to taste
- 1 tablespoon low-carb BBQ sauce
- 3 tablespoons whipping cream
- 1 lb. ground beef
- ½ lb. Italian sausage meat

Directions:

1. Preheat the oven to 350 degrees.
2. Spray a baking dish with non-stick oil.
3. Mix the flour and parmesan cheese in a bowl. Set aside.

4. Sauté onion, green pepper and garlic in the butter for 8 minutes.
5. Transfer the vegetables to a food processor and finely mince.
6. In a second bowl, whisk together the remaining ingredients except for the meat.
7. Use your hands to combine the beef and the sausage in a large bowl.
8. Add the egg/spice to the meat and use your hands to knead.
9. Mix in the flour and cheese mixture and combine thoroughly.
10. Place the meatloaf in the prepared baking dish.
11. Bake for an hour and let cool before slicing.
12. Serve with a steamed vegetable like cauliflower.

Dinner

Baked Salmon

2 servings

Ingredients:

- 4 tablespoons olive oil
- 2 minced garlic cloves
- 1 teaspoon basil
- 1 tablespoon parsley
- 2 tablespoon lemon juice
- Salt and pepper to taste
- 2 salmon fillets

Directions:

1. Place the salmon in a baking dish.
2. Combine all other ingredients and pour over the salmon.
3. Refrigerate for at least an hour.
4. Heat the oven to 375 degrees.
5. Transfer the salmon, with the marinade, to an aluminum foil pocket and wrap.
6. Bake for 40 minutes.

Day 22

(Daily: 11472 calories, 129g fat, 10.8g carbs, 85.5g protein)

Breakfast

Vanilla Smoothie

1 serving

Ingredients:

- 1/2 cup mascarpone cheese
- 3 egg yolks
- 5 ice cubes
- ¼ cup of water
- 2 tablespoon coconut oil
- ½ teaspoon vanilla
- 2 drops liquid stevia

Directions:

1. Place all ingredients in blender.
2. Pulse until the smoothie has a creamy consistency.
3. If desired, serve with whipped cream.

Lunch

2 servings

Cheese and Sausage Fries

Ingredients:

- 12 oz. breakfast sausage meat
- ¾ cup shredded cheddar cheese
- 12 small cheddar cubes
- 4 tablespoons butter

Directions:

1. Combine the sausage and shredded cheddar.
2. Section into 12 portions.
3. Insert 1 cheddar cube in the middle each sausage portion and form into a ball.
4. Melt the butter in a skillet and fry the sausages until they are crispy.
5. Serve with a large bowl of salad greens and low-carb dressing.

Dinner

Steak Fajitas

Serving - 4 fajitas – 1 serving

Ingredients for fajitas filling:

- 3 tablespoons diced onion
- 2 tablespoons diced bell pepper

- 1 diced jalapenos
- 2 tablespoons diced red chili pepper
- ¼ lb. of chuck or flank steak
- 3 tablespoons canned tomatoes
- 1 tablespoon ketchup
- Dash cider Vinegar
- 1/8 teaspoons minced garlic
- Dash liquid smoke
- Salt and pepper to taste

Ingredients for tortillas:

- 1/4 cup coconut flour
- 1 tbsp. ground psyllium husk
- 2 tablespoons butter
- 1/2 cup chicken broth
- Dash garlic powder
- Dash salt

Directions:

1. Dice all of the vegetables and peppers for the filing.
2. Place all ingredients in a large pot and lay the steak on top.
3. Simmer the fajita filing for 2-3 hours.
4. Shred the steak and set aside while you prepare the tortillas.
5. Bring the chicken broth to boil and add the remaining ingredients.
6. When the dough has formed, spread it out on a flat surface and cut small circles.
7. Fry the tortillas and fill with the steak mix.

Day 23

(Daily: 1282 calories, 48.7g fat, 18g carbs, 61.8g protein)

Breakfast

Waffles

2 Servings

Ingredient:

- 2 scoops vanilla protein powder
- 2 eggs
- 3 tablespoons melted butter
- Dash salt
- ½ cup sugar-free chocolate chips
- Sugar-free maple syrup

Directions:

1. Separate the eggs into yolks and whites.
2. Beat the egg whites until they are stiff.
3. Mix together the protein powder, yolks and butter and combine well.
4. Gently add the egg whites to the yolks along with a dash of salt.
5. Add the sugar-free chocolate chips and gently stir.
6. Transfer the batter to a waffle maker and cook the waffles according to directions.
7. Serve the waffles with the maple syrup.

Lunch

Salmon Patties

4 servings

Ingredients for Patties:

- 1 large can salmon
- 1 large egg
- 2 tablespoons mayonnaise
- 3 tablespoons grated parmesan
- Dash onion powder
- Salt and pepper to taste
- ¼ teaspoon Cajun seasoning
- Butter for frying

Ingredients for Sauce

- 1/3 cup mayonnaise
- 3 tablespoon mustard

Directions:

1. Mix together all of the salmon patty ingredients except for the butter.
2. Melt the butter in a skillet.
3. Form the salmon mixture into fairly large patties.
4. Brown the patties in batches for 4 minutes, turn them over, and fry the other side until browned.
5. Combine the sauce ingredients in a bowl and serve with the salmon patties.

Dinner

Chicken Salad with Walnuts

4 servings

Ingredients:

- 2 prepared chicken breasts
- 1 diced celery stalk
- ¼ chopped walnuts
- ¼ cup dried cranberries
- 1 avocado
- 1 tablespoon lemon juice
- Salt and pepper to taste

Directions:

1. Chop the chicken meat into bite-size pieces.
2. Add in the cranberries, celery and nuts.
3. Mash the avocado in another bowl and drizzle it with the lemon juice.
4. Fold the avocado into the chicken mix. Season to taste.

Day 24

(Daily: 1295 calories, 74.5g fat, 12.9g carbs, 71g protein)

Breakfast

1 serving

Eggs Poached in Tomato Sauce

Ingredients:

- 1 cup tomato sauce
- 1 diced chili pepper
- 2 large eggs
- 1 oz. feta cheese
- Salt and pepper to taste
- ½ teaspoon chopped basil

Directions:

1. Preheat oven to 400 degrees.
2. Heat the tomato sauce and chili pepper in a skillet.
3. Crack the eggs over the tomato sauce.
4. Top the eggs with salt, pepper and feta cheese.
5. With an oven mitt, slide the skillet into the oven.
6. Bake the eggs for 10 minutes.
7. Remove the eggs from oven and add the basil.

Lunch

2 servings

Thai Shrimp Curry

Ingredients:

- 3 tablespoons coconut oil
- 1 diced onion
- 1 diced garlic clove
- 1 cup coconut milk
- 1 cup vegetable stock
- 2 cups cooked shrimp
- 1 tablespoon green curry paste
- 1 cup broccoli florets
- 2 tablespoons chopped cilantro
- 2 teaspoons peanut butter
- 1 tablespoon soy sauce
- 1 tablespoon lime juice
- 1 tablespoon fish sauce
- 2 teaspoon grated ginger
- 1/4 teaspoon xanthan gum

Directions:

1. Heat the coconut oil in a large skillet and sauté the onion, ginger and garlic.
2. Mix in the green curry paste.
3. Stir in the soy sauce, fish sauce and peanut butter and blend.
4. Pour in the stock and coconut milk.
5. Simmer for 5 minutes, then stir in the xanthan gum.
6. Let the curry sauce thicken.

7. Add the broccoli and the cilantro.
8. Add in the shrimp and lime juice and stir.
9. Season with salt and pepper. If you want, you can stir in some sour cream before removing the skillet from the stove.

Dinner

Crockpot Pork Carnitas

Serves: 14

Ingredients:

- 6 lb. pork butt
- 3 tablespoon butter
- 1 sliced onion
- 1 tablespoon cumin
- 1 tablespoon thyme
- 2 tablespoon chili powder
- Salt and pepper to taste
- 4 diced garlic clove
- 1 cup water

Directions:

1. Rub butter on the inside of a slow cooker.
2. Place the sliced onion in the slow cooker.
3. Layer the onion with the garlic.
4. Cut a few notches into the fatty part of the meat.
5. Combine all the spices and rub the paste onto the entire butt.
6. Transfer the butt to the slow cooker and add a cup of water.

7. The meat is done when it falls apart.
8. Serve the meat with sliced tomatoes and cucumbers drizzled with non-carb dressing.

Day 25

(Daily: 1396 calories, 149.5g fat, 25.8g carbs, 54.4g protein)

Breakfast

Eggs with Spinach

2 servings

Ingredients:

- 1 cup plain Greek yogurt
- Salt and pepper to taste
- 2 tablespoons unsalted butter, divided
- 2 tablespoons olive oil
- ¼ cup chopped leeks
- 2 chopped scallion
- 8 cups baby spinach
- 1 teaspoon lemon juice
- 5 large eggs
- 1/4 teaspoon red pepper flakes

Direction:

1. In a bowl, add the garlic and salt to the yogurt. Set aside.
2. Preheat oven to 300 degrees.
3. Heat the butter and sauté the scallion and leek for 8 minutes.
4. Mix in the spinach and drizzle in the lemon juice and continue stirring for 5 minutes.
5. Crack the eggs into the spinach.
6. Place the skillet in the oven and bake for 12 minutes.

7. Remove the skillet from oven, spoon the yogurt over the eggs.

Lunch

Stuffed Avocado

2 servings

Ingredients:

- 2 large eggs
- 2 tablespoons diced onion
- 1 diced celery stalk
- 1 tablespoon mayonnaise
- ½ teaspoon lime juice
- ½ teaspoon mustard
- Dash of hot sauce
- Salt and Pepper to taste
- 1 avocado

Direction:

1. Boil the eggs in a small pan for 10 minutes.
2. Use a food processor to chop the eggs.
3. Add all ingredients except the avocado to a bowl and thoroughly combine.
4. Slice the avocado open and remove the pit.
5. Distribute the egg salad into the avocado holes.

Dinner

Tuna Melt

2 servings

Ingredients:

- 1 can albacore tuna
- ¼ cup mayonnaise
- 1 diced avocado
- 1/3 cup almond flour
- 1/3 cup parmesan cheese
- ¼ teaspoon garlic powder
- Salt and Pepper to Taste
- Coconut oil for frying

Directions:

1. Drain the tuna and transfer to a large bowl.
2. Add all remaining ingredients except for the avocado and almond flour and combine well.
3. Mush the avocado meat and add to the bowl.
4. Form the ingredients into ball and dredge through the flour.
5. Heat the coconut oil in a skillet and fry the tuna balls until they are crisp.

Day 26

(Daily: 1528 calories, 75.2g fat, 11g carbs, 98.2g protein)

Breakfast

Spinach and Mushroom Quiche

Serves: 6

Ingredients:

- 1 ½ cups sliced mushrooms
- 10 oz. frozen spinach that has been thawed
- 1 tablespoon butter
- 1 minced garlic clove
- 4 eggs
- 1 cup milk
- 1/3 cup grated parmesan
- ½ cup shredded mozzarella
- 3 oz. feta cheese
- Salt & pepper to taste

Directions:

1. Preheat the oven to 350 degrees.
2. Squeeze all moisture from the spinach.
3. Sauté the garlic in the butter for a few minutes.
4. Add the mushrooms and continue cooking for 5 minutes.
5. Coat a baking dish with more butter or a non-stick spray.
6. Transfer the spinach to the dish, top with the mushrooms and the feta cheese.

7. Whisk the eggs, milk and the parmesan in a bowl and add the salt and pepper.
8. Pour the mixture into the baking dish.
9. Add the mozzarella.
10. Bake the quiche for 50 minutes. Cut into slices.

Dinner

Stuffed Pork Chops

Serves: 4

Ingredients:

- 4 thick pork chops
- 3 oz. blue cheese
- 4 oz. feta cheese
- 3 chopped scallions
- 3 oz. cream cheese
- Salt and pepper to taste
- 1 tablespoon butter or bacon fat

Directions:

1. Preheat oven to 350 degrees.
2. Combine the cheeses in a bowl and add the scallions and cream cheese. Mix well.
3. Use a sharp knife to open one side of the chops
4. Spoon the cheese mix into the chop.
5. If necessary, seal the opening using a toothpick.
6. Season with salt and pepper.
7. Heat the butter or bacon fat and sear the pork chops on both sides.

8. Place the chops in a baking dish and bake for 50 minutes.
9. Serve with Broccoli Slaw.

Day 27

(Daily: 1630 calories, 57.5g fat, 21.4g carbs, 66.2g protein)

Breakfast

Ham and Cheese Muffin

4 servings

Ingredients:

- 6 large eggs
- 3 oz. Brie cheese
- 3 oz. diced ham
- 1/3 cup salsa
- ½ cup chopped cremini mushrooms
- Salt and Pepper to taste

Directions:

1. Preheat the oven to 350 degrees.
2. Lightly butter a muffin pan.
3. In a bowl, use a fork to mush the Brie.
4. Whisk the eggs with the cheese.
5. Add in the remaining ingredients and mix.
6. Spoon the batter into the muffin pan.
7. Bake the muffins for 25 minutes.

Lunch

Easy Salad

1 serving

Ingredients:

- 2 tomatoes
- 1 avocado
- 6 unpitted olives – any kind
- 3 oz. mozzarella cheese
- 1 tablespoon pesto
- 2 tablespoon olive oil
- Salt and pepper to taste

Directions:

1. Slide the tomatoes and avocado; cut the olives in half.
2. Place the tomatoes, avocado and olives in a bowl.
3. Top with small mozzarella pieces and pesto.
4. Drizzle with the olive oil and season with salt and pepper.

Dinner

Corned Beef and Cabbage Rolls

Ingredients:

- 4- lb. corned beef brisket
- 15 cabbage leaves
- 1 diced onion

- 1/4 cup beef broth
- 1/4 cup red wine
- 1 tablespoon butter
- 1 tablespoon mustard
- 1 teaspoon salt
- 1 teaspoon peppercorns
- 1 teaspoon mustard seeds
- 2 teaspoon Worcestershire sauce
- 1/4 teaspoon Allspice
- 1 bay leaf

Direction:

1. Place the brisket in a slow cooker.
2. Add all of the spices.
3. Add the beef broth and wine. Stir.
4. Cook on low for 6-7 hours.
5. Just prior to the brisket being done, bring a large pot of water to boil.
6. Cook 15 cabbage leaves for 3 minutes.
7. Immediately place the leaves in cold water.
8. Boil the onion slices in the same water until they are soft.
9. Transfer the brisket to a platter and slice the meat.
10. Lay a cabbage leaf flat and fill with beef and onions.
11. Roll up the cabbage leaf and tuck in the ends.
12. Repeat with the remaining leaves.

Day 27

(Daily: 1922 calories, 117g fat, 9.5g carbs, 131g protein)

Breakfast

Smoked Salmon Scrambled Eggs

Serving 1

Ingredients:

- 1 tablespoons butter
- 2 cups salad greens
- 2 large eggs
- 3 tablespoons whipping cream
- 2 oz. smoked salmon
- 1 oz. cream cheese
- Salt and pepper to taste

Directions:

1. Whisk together the eggs and the cream.
2. In a skillet, melt the butter. When it starts to smoke, stir in the eggs.
3. Keep moving the eggs around until they are fluffy.
4. Place the salad greens on a plate. Top with the scrambled eggs.
5. Add the smoked salmon on top of the eggs and place the cream cheese on the side.

Lunch

Sesame Chicken

2 servings

Ingredients:

- 1 cup broccoli florets
- 1 egg
- 1 tablespoon corn starch
- 4 cut up chicken thighs
- 2 tablespoons sesame seed oil
- Salt and pepper to taste

Ingredients for Sauce:

- 2 tablespoons soy sauce
- 1 tablespoon sesame oil
- 2 tablespoons brown sugar or Sukrin Gold
- 2 teaspoon rice vinegar
- 1 teaspoon grated ginger
- 1 diced garlic clove
- 1 tablespoon sesame seeds
- ½ corn starch

Directions:

1. Whisk the eggs with the cornstarch.
2. Coat the chicken pieces with the egg.
3. Let the chicken sit for 15 minutes.
4. Put the broccoli in a pan of water and cook.
5. Heat the sesame seed oil in a skillet and fry the chicken in batches.

6. Prepare the sauce by combining all of the sauce ingredients.
7. When the chicken is done, pour the sesame sauce into the skillet and stir to coat the chicken.
8. Cook for about 5 minutes.
9. Place the cooked broccoli on a platter.
10. Transfer the chicken on top of the broccoli.

Note: You can make more broccoli to have enough for dinner.

Dinner

Roast Rib

8 Servings

Ingredients:

- 5 lbs. rib roast
- Salt and pepper to taste
- 1 teaspoon garlic powder

Directions:

1. Season the roast with the spices.
2. Let the meat sit on the counter for about an hour.
3. Preheat the oven to 375 degrees.
4. Place the roast in the oven and cook for an hour.
5. Turn off the heat, but leave the roast in the oven for another 3 hours.
6. Turn the oven back to 375 degrees and roast the meat for another 40 minutes.
7. Let the roast sit for 15 minutes before serving.

8. Serve with a side of broccoli.

Day 28

(Daily: 1223 calories, 97.4g fat, 17.5g carbs, 51.2g protein)

Breakfast

Strawberry Smoothie

1 serving

Ingredients:

- 1/3 cup coconut milk
- ½ cup almond milk
- ½ cup strawberries, preferable fresh
- 1 tablespoon coconut oil
- ¼ teaspoon vanilla extract
- 3 drops stevia
- 1 teaspoon chia seeds
- Optionally: whipped cream

Directions:

1. Place all ingredients except for the chia seeds and whipped cream in a blender and mix until smooth.
2. Pour in a large glass. Add the chia seeds. If desired, top with whipped cream.

Lunch

Chili Con Carne

5 servings

Ingredients:

- 1 lb. hamburger meat
- 1 lb. Italian sausage meat
- 2 diced green peppers
- 1 diced onion
- 1 medium can tomato sauce
- 2 tablespoons chili powder
- 1 tablespoon unsweetened cocoa powder
- 1 tablespoon cumin
- 1 tablespoon coconut oil
- 2 diced garlic cloves
- 1 tablespoon butter
- Salt and pepper to taste

Directions:

1. Melt the butter in a skillet.
2. Sauté the green pepper, onion and garlic.
3. Place the ground beef and sausage in a large pan and brown evenly.
4. Add the green pepper, onion and garlic to the meat and season with salt and pepper.
5. Mix in the remaining ingredients and stir well.
6. Cook for 30 minutes, then simmer for another hour or more.
7. If desired, serve with sour cream and shredded cheese.

Chicken Cordon Bleu with Green Beans

4 servings

Ingredients:

- 2 skinless, boneless chicken breasts
- 2 oz. Swiss cheese
- 4 ham slices
- 4 bacon slices
- Toothpicks

Directions:

1. Split the chicken breasts in half.
2. Lay the chicken flat, in butterfly fashion.
3. Place 2 slices of ham and 1 slice of cheese on top of each chicken breast.
4. Fold the chicken up, with the ham and cheese inside.
5. Wrap each chicken breast in a slice of bacon.
6. Use toothpicks to hold the chicken together.
7. Transfer the chicken breast to a greased baking dish.
8. Heat the oven to 325 degrees.
9. Bake the chicken for 45 minutes.
10. Serve with green beans.

Roasted Green Beans

4 servings

Ingredients:

- 1 lb. fresh green beans
- 4 tablespoons olive oil

- 1/2 cup chopped pecans
- 1/3 cup parmesan cheese
- Zest of 1 lemon
- 1 minced garlic clove
- 1 teaspoon red pepper flakes

Direction:

1. Preheat the oven to 450 degrees.
2. Place the green beans in a bowl and add the o.
3. Add the other ingredients and mix well.
4. Place everything in a baking dish and roast for 25 minutes.
5. Serve with the Cordon Bleu.

Day 29

(Daily: 1349 calories, 92.9g fat, 14.7g carbs, 92.1g protein)

Breakfast

6 servings

Veggie Sausage Bake

Ingredients:

- 1 lb. breakfast sausage
- 2 cups shredded green cabbage
- 2 cups diced eggplant
- ½ cup diced onion
- 3 eggs
- 2 cups shredded cheddar cheese
- ½ cup mayonnaise
- 2 teaspoon yellow mustard
- 1 teaspoon sage
- Dash of pepper

Directions:

1. Preheat the oven to 375 degrees.
2. Butter a baking dish or casserole dish.
3. Sear the sausage meat, but don't cook it entirely.
4. Add the eggplant, cabbage, and onion to the sausage and cook until the sausage is fully done.
5. Transfer the mixture to the baking dish.
6. Whisk together the mayonnaise, eggs and seasoning to a smooth consistency.

7. Stir in 1 cup of cheddar cheese.
8. Pour the egg/cheese mix on top of the sausage mix.
9. Add the second cup of cheese on top.
10. Bake the casserole for 30 minutes.

Lunch

Chicken Quesadilla

1 serving:

Ingredients:

- 4 oz. pepper jack cheese
- 3 oz. cooked chicken meat
- 3 avocado slices
- 1 teaspoon chopped jalapeño
- 1 low carb tortilla
- 1/4 teaspoon red pepper
- 1/4 teaspoon garlic powder
- Salt and pepper to taste

Directions:

1. Shred the chicken meat.
2. Fry the tortilla.
3. Place the cheese, shredded chicken, avocado onto half of the wrap.
4. Add the jalapeno cheese and the spices
5. Fold the tortilla in half and press on the edges with your fingers to tighten.
6. Remove the quesadilla and enjoy with sour cream or salsa.

Dinner

Ginger Beef

2 servings

Ingredients:

- 2 sirloin steaks sliced into thin strips
- 1 tablespoon olive oil
- 2 small diced tomatoes
- 3 diced scallions
- 1 minced garlic clove
- 1 diced red chili
- 1 teaspoon ground ginger
- 4 tablespoons apple cider vinegar
- Salt and pepper

Directions:

1. Heat the oil and sear the steaks in a skillet.
2. Add the tomatoes, onion and garlic.
3. Use a bowl to mix the vinegar with the remaining seasoning.
4. Spoon into the skillet and simmer until there is no liquid left.
5. Serve with a simple salad.

Day 30

(Daily: 1218 calories, 39.5g fat, 11g carbs, 52.7g protein)

Breakfast

Banana Crepes

1serving

Ingredients:

- 3 tablespoons almond flour
- 1 teaspoon flaxseed
- 2 large eggs
- 3 tablespoons almond milk
- 1 tablespoon stevia
- 1/8 teaspoon nutmeg
- 1/8 teaspoon allspice
- ¼ teaspoon vanilla
- Dash of salt
- 1 tablespoon sugar-free chocolate chips and half a sliced banana for topping.

Directions:

1. Place all ingredients except for the topping in a food processor and pulse until the batter is smooth.
2. Coat a crepe pan with non-stick spray and pour in the batter.
3. Spread the batter evenly so that it's nice and thin.
4. Cook for 3 minutes or until the bottom is browned.
5. For topping, melt the chocolate in a microwave.

6. Top the crepe with the banana slices and drizzle it with the chocolate chips.

Lunch

Baked Chicken

Ingredients:

- 2 tablespoons olive oil
- 2 chicken breasts
- ½ teaspoon brown mustard
- ½ teaspoon minced garlic
- 2 tablespoons almond flour

Directions:

1. Preheat the oven to 375 degrees.
2. Cover the bottom of a baking dish with the olive oil.
3. Place the chicken on top/
4. Rub the chicken with the mustard and garlic.
5. Dust the chicken with the almond flour.
6. Bake for 35-40 minutes.

Dinner

Portobello Pizza

Serves: 1

Ingredients:

- 1 Portobello mushroom cap
- 1 tablespoon olive oil

- 2 tablespoon tomato sauce
- ¼ cup shredded mozzarella cheese
- 1 cooked and sliced chicken sausage
- 1 tablespoon chopped basil

Directions:

1. Brush the Portobello cap with the oil and warm in a skillet or on a grill with the back down. Season with the salt and pepper.
2. Add the tomato sauce, cheese and sausage to the cap.
3. Cook until the mozzarella is melted.
4. Top with the chopped basil.

Keto Snacks To Go

Enjoy two of these tasty treat each day.

1. Coffee with cream
2. Pork rinds
3. 2 slices of cheese
4. Handful of nuts
5. Tomatoes and cucumbers
6. Handful of berries
7. Baked vegetable crisps
8. Handful of seeds
9. Hummus dips
10. 2 pieces of 80 percent cocoa chocolate pieces
11. 2 celery stalks with peanut butter spread
12. 3-4 slices of avocado
13. 1 hard-boiled egg
14. Pepperoni slices
15. Handful of olives

Thank you again for purchasing this book, I hope you enjoyed reading it as much as I enjoyed writing it for you!

Finally, if you enjoyed this book, I'd like to ask you to leave a review on Amazon, it would be greatly appreciated!

All my best,

Sarah Underwood

Made in the USA
Lexington, KY
03 August 2019